中国交通名片丛书

RURAL ROADS IN CHINA

中国"四好农村路"

《中国"四好农村路"》编写组

人民交通出版社

北京

新时代新征程，要持续发力，久久为功，进一步完善政策法规，提高治理能力，实施好新一轮农村公路提升行动，持续推动"四好农村路"高质量发展，助力宜居宜业和美乡村建设，为促进农民农村共同富裕、推进乡村全面振兴、加快农业农村现代化步伐、推进中国式现代化提供坚强服务保障。

——习近平对进一步做好"四好农村路"建设作出重要指示强调
持续发力久久为功　推动"四好农村路"高质量发展
《人民日报》2024年5月30日01版

In the new era and new journey, we must maintain sustained efforts, and strive for long-term success in further refining policies and regulations, enhancing governance capabilities, effectively implementing a new round of rural road improvement initiatives, continuously promoting the high-quality development of the construction, management, maintenance and operation of roads in rural areas. We should contribute to the construction of livable, business-friendly, and beautiful villages, provide strong service guarantees for promoting common prosperity in rural areas and among farmers, advancing comprehensive rural revitalization, accelerating the pace of agricultural and rural modernization, and advancing the path to Chinese-style modernization.

Xi Jinping made important instructions on further improving the construction, management, maintenance and operation of roads in rural areas and emphasized maintaining sustained efforts and striving for long-term success in promoting the high-quality development of the construction, management, maintenance and operation of roads in rural areas

People's Daily, May 30, 2024, Page 01

前 言

2021年10月，习近平总书记在联合国第二届全球可持续交通大会开幕式上的主旨讲话中指出，新中国成立以来，几代人逢山开路、遇水架桥，建成了交通大国，正在加快建设交通强国。

今日中国，公路成网，铁路密布，高铁飞驰，巨轮远航，飞机翱翔，邮路畅通，高速铁路、高速公路、城市轨道交通、港口万吨级泊位等规模均跃居世界第一。中国高铁、中国路、中国桥、中国港、中国快递成为亮丽的"中国名片"。

2014年3月，习近平总书记对"四好农村路"首次作出重要批示。10年来，"四好农村路"建设取得了历史性成就，截至2023年底，农村公路总里程达到460万公里，实施农村公路危桥改造5.8万座、安全生命防护工程123万公里，农村开通了客货邮融合线路1.1万余条，农村客车年代运邮件快件超过2亿件，全国具备条件的乡镇和建制村全部通硬化路、通客车、通邮路。这10年，是农村公路网络持续延伸、通达程度大幅提高的10年，是农村公路管理养护持续升级、农村出行条件大为改善的10年，是农村公路运输服务持续优化、服务品质稳步提升的10年。农村公路已经成为老百姓家门口的致富路、幸福路、连心路、振兴路。

我们编写出版《中国"四好农村路"》一书，按照致富路、幸福路、连心路、振兴路编排，以图文并茂的形式集中勾勒、展现中国"四好农村路"发展取得的突出成就。

翻开本书，我们可以深刻感受到：一条条通城达乡的"四好农村路"，盘活了农村特色资源，带动了农村经济发展，成为农村地区摆脱贫困、实现小康、走向富裕的致富路；一条条进村入户的"四好农村路"，改善了乡村的人居环境，融合了城市文明与乡村文化，展现了乡路与村景相得益彰的和美画卷，成为农民阔步美好生活的幸福路；一条条穿山越岭的"四好农村路"，解决了千百年来困扰农村出行的难题，沟通了中国农村的东西南北，为当地百姓带来了发展机遇与希望，成为凝聚民心的连心路；一条条纵横交错的"四好农村路"，串联起千家万户，织就了铺陈在广袤中国大地上的农村公路网，为乡村振兴注入了活力动能，成为助推农业农村现代化的振兴路。

奋进新征程，我们要坚持以习近平新时代中国特色社会主义思想为指导，深入学习贯彻习近平总书记关于"四好农村路"的重要指示精神，持续发力，久久为功，持续推动"四好农村路"高质量发展，助力宜居宜业和美乡村建设，为促进农民农村共同富裕、推进乡村全面振兴、加快农业农村现代化步伐、推进中国式现代化提供坚强服务保障。

编者

2024年9月

PREFACE

In October 2021, President Xi Jinping delivered a keynote speech at the opening ceremony of the Second United Nations Global Sustainable Transport Conference, pointing out that since the founding of New China, generation after generation of the Chinese people have worked in the spirit of opening roads through mountains and putting bridges over rivers, and turned China into a country with vast transport infrastructure. Today, Chinese people are redoubling efforts to build China into a country with great transport strength.

China has already built a huge network of highways, railways, ships, airplanes and express delivery routes. China ranks first in the world in terms of the scale of high-speed railways, expressways, urban rail transit, and ports with 10,000-ton berths. China's high-speed railways, roads, bridges, ports and express delivery have become shining "business cards of China".

In March 2014, for the first time, General Secretary Xi Jinping made important instructions on the construction, management, maintenance and operation of roads in rural areas. Over the past ten years, China has made historic achievements in the construction, management, maintenance and operation of roads in rural areas. As of the end of 2023, the total mileage of rural roads had reached 4.60 million kilometers, 58,000 dangerous bridges on rural roads had been rebuilt and 1.23 million kilometers of road safety and life protection projects had been implemented. Over 11,000 integrated passenger, freight, and postal routes were opened in rural areas, and over 200 million mail and express deliveries were transported annually by rural buses. All qualified townships and administrative villages across the country had access to paved roads, passenger buses, and postal routes. These ten years have witnessed the continuous expansion of the rural road network and a significant improvement in accessibility. They have also been marked by the continuous upgrading of rural road management and maintenance, leading to significant improvement in rural travel conditions. Furthermore, the transportation services on rural roads have been continuously optimized, with a steady improvement in service quality. Rural roads have become roads of prosperity, happiness, unity, and revitalization right at people's doorsteps.

We have compiled and published the book "Rural Roads in China". The book is organized according to the themes of "wealth creation road", "happiness road", "heart connection road", and "revitalization road". In the form of illustrations and texts, the book focuses on outlining and displaying the outstanding achievements made in the construction, management, maintenance and operation of rural roads in China.

Through reading this book, we can deeply sense the profound impact of the rural roads: these roads, connecting cities to villages, have revitalized distinctive rural resources, driven rural economic development, and become the path to prosperity for rural areas to get rid of poverty, achieve moderate prosperity, and move towards affluence; these roads, leading into villages and households, have improved the living environment in rural areas, integrated urban civilization with rural culture, and presented a harmonious picture of rural roads and village scenery, becoming the path to happiness for farmers to stride towards a better life; these roads, traversing mountains and valleys, have solved the difficult problem of rural travel that has plagued people for thousands of years, connected the east, west, north, and south of rural China, and brought development opportunities and hope to local people, becoming the path to solidarity to unite the people's hearts; these crisscrossing rural roads have connected thousands of households, formed a rural road network across the vast land of China, and injected vitality into rural revitalization, becoming the path to revitalization that promotes agricultural and rural modernization.

As we embark on the new journey, we must adhere to the guidance of Xi Jinping Thought on Socialism with Chinese Characteristics for a New Era, thoroughly study and implement the important instructions of General Secretary Xi Jinping on the construction, management, maintenance and operation of roads in rural areas, maintain sustained efforts, and strive for long-term success in continuously promoting the high-quality development of the rural roads. We should contribute to the construction of livable, business-friendly, and beautiful villages, provide strong service guarantees for promoting common prosperity in rural areas and among farmers, advancing comprehensive rural revitalization, accelerating the pace of agricultural and rural modernization, and advancing the Chinese modernization drive.

Editors
September 2024

目 录　CONTENTS

P001 **致富路** WEALTH CREATION ROAD	**P049** **幸福路** HAPPINESS ROAD
P099 **连心路** HEART CONNECTION ROAD	**P143** **振兴路** REVITALIZATION ROAD

中国
"四好农村路"
RURAL ROADS IN
CHINA

致富路

WEALTH CREATION ROAD

以前，进村的羊肠小道弯弯曲曲，遇到雨雪天气就是满地泥巴，两个轮的架子车都没法通过。如今的梁家河村，沟峁塬亲密"牵手"，山上的7个村民小组也被14公里的环山公路连成了一处。梁家河村农村公路，让这个偏僻的小村庄走向开放、拥抱变革，让"梁家河"苹果走向全国，让梁家河村日子越来越红火，村子越来越美丽。

In the past, the road leading to the village was winding, and when it rained or snowed, it was full of mud. Thanks to the rural road, people in Liangjiahe village are living better and better, and the village is becoming more and more beautiful.

陕西省延安市延川县文安驿镇梁家河村农村公路
Rural Road in Liangjiahe Village, Wen'anyi Town, Yanchuan County, Yan'an City, Shaanxi Province

北京市门头沟区农村公路
Rural Road in Mentougou District, Beijing Municipality

WEALTH CREATION ROAD 致富路

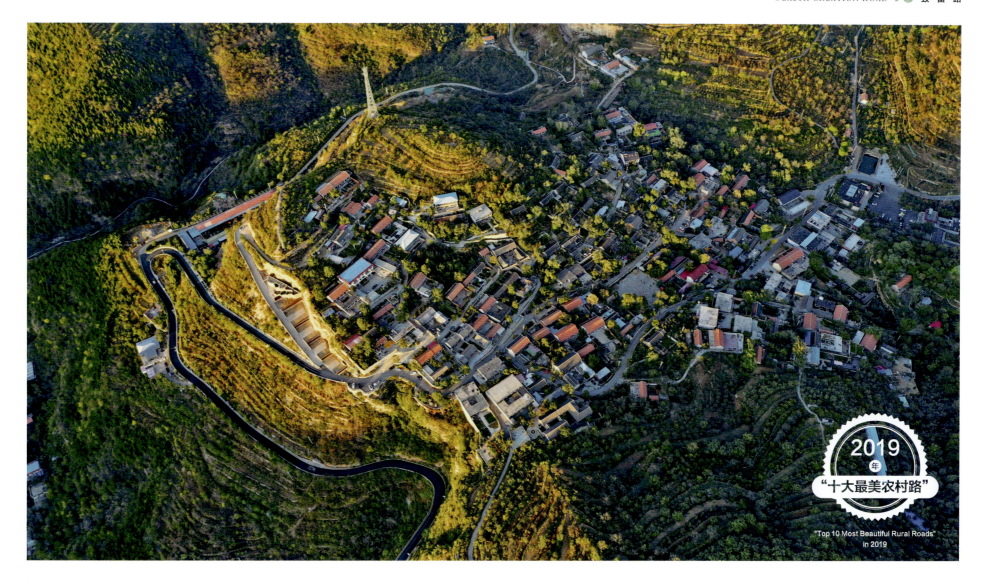

西井峪村四面环山，绿树蔽舍，花果飘香，具有因石而生、因石而居、因石而乐的古朴遗风。西井峪路带动了人流物流信息流，带动了人民生活水平提高，带动了当地旅游业的大发展，实现了"修一条公路、富一方百姓"的乘数效应。

Xijingyu Road has driven the flow of people, logistics and information, improved people's living standards, and led to the development of local tourism, realizing the multiplier effect of "building a highway, enriching local people".

天津市蓟州区渔阳镇西井峪路
Xijingyu Road in Yuyang Town, Jizhou District, Tianjin Municipality

河北省邯郸市涉县圣福天路
Shengfu "Sky Road" in Shexian County, Handan City, Hebei Province

"Top 10 Most Beautiful Rural Roads" in 2019

圣福天路创新性地提出七条生态修路原则，让路和自然和谐共生，是打通河北邯郸涉县中部和北部的一条风景旅游通道，也是吸引八方游客、带动当地旅游经济发展的致富路。

Shengfu "Sky Road" innovatively puts forward seven ecological road construction principles to make the road and nature in harmony. It's not only a scenic tourism corridor, but also a wealth creation road which attracts tourists from all directions and drives the local tourism economy development.

WEALTH CREATION ROAD　　致 富 路

阜平县农村公路将沟与沟连接起来，形成网状交通格局，在方便群众出行的同时，还发展成为产业路、旅游路，绘就了一幅幅路通百业兴的恢弘画卷。

Rural road in Fuping county connects ditch with the ditch to form a mesh transportation pattern, which facilitates people's travelling and at the same time develops into an industry road and tourism road.

河北省保定市阜平县农村公路
Rural Road in Fuping County, Baoding City, Hebei Province

中国"四好农村路"　RURAL ROADS IN CHINA

2021年"我家门口那条路——最具人气的路"

"The Road in Front of My House —The Most Popular Road" in 2021

空中俯瞰，兴县沿黄扶贫旅游公路如蛟龙盘踞，气势恢宏，又如玉带环绕，百转千回。它孕育于红色文化中，开辟于青山绿水间，蜿蜒于蓝天白云下，形成了景在路中、路在景中、路景一体的优美画卷。

From the aerial view, the tourism road for poverty alleviation along the Yellow River in Xingxian county looks like a coiled dragon, and also a jade belt. It was bred in the red culture, opened up in green mountains and clear waters, winding under the blue sky and white clouds, forming a beautiful picture with landscape and road in harmony.

山西省吕梁市兴县沿黄扶贫旅游公路

Tourism Road for Poverty Alleviation along the Yellow River in Xingxian County, Lvliang City, Shanxi Province

WEALTH CREATION ROAD　致 富 路

山西省运城市垣曲县毛家镇农村公路
Rural Road in Maojia Town, Yuanqu County, Yuncheng City, Shanxi Province

"The Road in Front of My House
—The Most Popular Road" in 2022

内蒙古自治区鄂尔多斯市鄂托克前旗昂素至城川红色旅游公路
Red Tourism Road from Angsu to Chengchuan in Otog Front Banner, Ordos City, Inner Mongolia Autonomous Region

昂素至城川红色旅游公路穿越沙漠、横跨草原，有效串联了马良诚、顾寿山烈士纪念园，红色秘密交通站，阳早寒春三边牧场陈列馆，延安民族学院城川纪念馆，以及多处农牧产业示范基地，切实带动了沿线红色旅游产业发展。

The red tourism road from Angsu to Chengchuan spreads through the desert and crosses the grassland, and effectively promotes the development of red tourism industry along the route.

内蒙古自治区兴安盟乌兰浩特市农村公路
Rural Road in Ulanhot City, Xing'an League,
Inner Mongolia Autonomous Region

"Top 10 Most Beautiful Rural Roads"
in 2023

辽宁省大连市普兰店区快二线
The Second Fast Road in Pulandian District, Dalian City,
Liaoning Province

吉林省延边朝鲜族自治州安图县农村公路

Rural Road in Antu County, Yanbian Korean Autonomous Prefecture, Jilin Province

黑龙江省牡丹江市东宁市农村公路
Rural Road in Dongning City, Mudanjiang City, Heilongjiang Province

中国"四好农村路" RURAL ROADS IN CHINA

上海市宝山区罗迎路

Luoying Road in Baoshan District, Shanghai Municipality

WEALTH CREATION ROAD　致 富 路

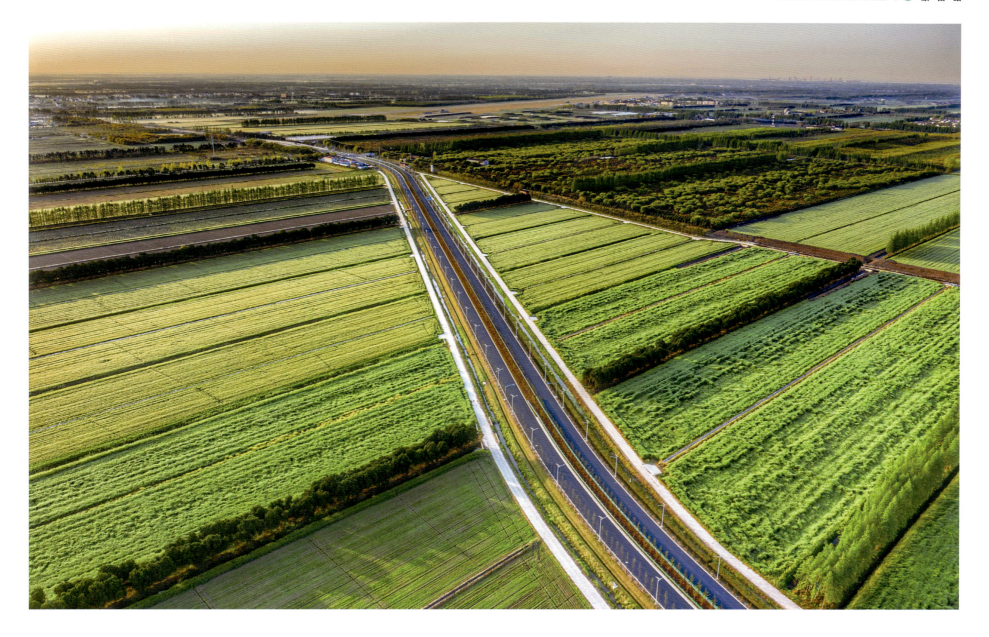

上海市崇明区北沿公路

Beiyan Road in Chongming District, Shanghai Municipality

江苏省泰州市兴化千垛美路
Qianduomei Road in Xinghua City, Taizhou City, Jiangsu Province

江苏省无锡市农村公路
Rural Road in Wuxi City, Jiangsu Province

"Top 10 Most Beautiful Rural Roads" in 2019

和合环线在路域整治上，做到"嘉者收之、俗者屏之、乱者统之"；在环境协调上，做到"旧而不破、简而不陋、野而不荒"。它串起了山水林田湖，串起了城镇乡村景，打通了"绿水青山"转化为"金山银山"的大通途。

Hehe ring road strings up the mountains, waters, forests, fields and lakes. Through this road, clear waters and green mountains are turning into invaluable assets.

浙江省台州市天台县寒山和合环线
Hanshan Hehe Ring Road in Tiantai County, Taizhou City, Zhejiang Province

2022年 "十大最美农村路"
"Top 10 Most Beautiful Rural Roads" in 2022

浙江省绍兴市柯桥区平王线
Pingwang Road in Keqiao District, Shaoxing City, Zhejiang Province

平王线，深植会稽山腹地，路况卓越，设施完善，融合自然古韵。它不仅是通行之道，更是旅游热线，串联山水美景与人文古迹，成为骑行天堂。智慧管理，服务齐全，沿线经济因路而兴，乡村因路而美，村民因路而富。

Pingwang Road, deeply rooted in the hinterland of Kuaiji Mountain, has excellent road conditions, perfect facilities and natural ancient charm. It is not only a way to pass through, but also a hot line for tourism, linking the beautiful scenery and humanistic monuments, becoming a cycling paradise. With intelligent management and complete services, the economy along the route has prospered, the villages have become beautiful, and the villagers have become rich.

浙江省丽水市龙泉市西独线
Xidu Road in Longquan City, Lishui City, Zhejiang Province

西独线是一条生态休闲、产业兴旺、文旅融合、红色传承之路，串起了白云岩景区、下樟古村等旅游景点。古村常年云雾缭绕、幽若仙谷，为西独线增添了得天独厚的生态美景。

Xidu Road is a road that integrates ecological leisure, industry prosperity, cultural tourism, and red heritage. It strings up the Baiyunyan scenic spot, Xiazhang ancient village and other tourist attractions. The ancient village adds unique ecological beauty to Xidu Road.

曲折盘旋、绕山而上的梅汤路与山区地形地貌深度融合,在大别山腹地的莲花峰上实现了由"羊肠小道"到"康庄大道"的华丽嬗变,成为"中国红岭公路"最险最美路段。

Meitang Road integrates deeply with the topography and landscape in the mountainous area. It's the most dangerous and beautiful road located in the hinterland of the Dabie Mountains.

安徽省六安市金寨县 X324 梅汤路

X324 Meitang Road in Jinzhai County, Lu'an City, Anhui Province

2020年"十大最美农村路"

"Top 10 Most Beautiful Rural Roads" in 2020

福建省宁德市霞浦县农村公路
Rural Road in Xiapu County,
Ningde City, Fujian Province

霞浦县农村公路融合了优美的山海自然旅游资源与独特的人文旅游资源，彰显"山海画境，行摄霞浦"的形象意境，极大方便了沿线群众的生产生活，通过它将金刚虾、大黄鱼、生蚝等当地特色产品销往各地，从根本上解决了沿线村庄通行难和运输不畅等问题。

The rural road in Xiapu county integrates beautiful natural tourism resources and the unique human tourism resources, greatly facilitating the production and life of the people along the route. The problem of poor transportation in the villages along the route has been fundamentally solved.

中国"四好农村路" RURAL ROADS IN CHINA

福建省三明市尤溪县农村公路
Rural Road in Youxi County, Sanming City, Fujian Province

江西省赣州市会昌县文武坝镇至富城乡农村公路
Rural Road from Wenwuba Town to Fucheng Township, Huichang County, Ganzhou City, Jiangxi Province

山东省临沂市郯城县许家湖—重坊环线
Xujiahu-Chongfang Ring Road in Tancheng County, Linyi City, Shandong Province

许家湖—重坊环线是一条独具特色的乡村旅游路，沿途有郯国古城、中华银杏品种园、银杏古梅园等特色景点，步步皆风景、处处美如画，同时也是一条名副其实的强村富民路，银杏产品交互供应，琅琊草帽享誉盛名，带动万家富。

Xujiahu-Chongfang ring road is a unique rural tourism road with characteristic attractions such as Tancheng ancient city, Chinese ginkgo varieties garden, and ginkgo ancient plum garden. It's worthy of the name of the wealth creation road.

山东省烟台市招远市欧家夼—邱家（欧邱线）
Oujiakuang-Qiujia (Ouqiu) Road in Zhaoyuan City, Yantai City, Shandong Province

"Top 10 Most Beautiful Rural Roads" in 2019

河南省洛阳市栾川县伊源路
Yiyuan Road in Luanchuan County, Luoyang City, Henan Province

伊源路通过近水亲水、观山赏景、增设休憩服务设施、拓展沿线产业生态，将景观、人文资源有机贯通，是展示"旅游扶贫"的成果之路、支撑"康养度假"的生态之路、实现"乡村振兴"的产业之路。

Yiyuan Road is an organic link between landscape and human resources through additional setting of leisure service facilities, and expansion of industry ecology along the route. It is the road to show the results of "poverty alleviation through tourism", the ecological road to support "recreation and vacation" and the industry road to realize "rural revitalization".

河南省洛阳市新安县农村公路
Rural Road in Xin'an County, Luoyang City, Henan Province

湖北省黄冈市蕲春县绿唐线
Lvtang Road in Qichun County, Huanggang City, Hubei Province

　　绿唐线是三角山风景区与外界对接的主要交通要道，沿线自然景观、人文风光相得益彰。在它的辐射带动下，蕲艾、黄精、射干等特色产业蓬勃发展，对蕲春县株林镇交通出行、美丽乡村建设、产业振兴、旅游开发、脱贫攻坚等具有决定性作用，是一条名副其实的民生路、旅游路、致富路。

Lvtang Road is the main traffic road between the Sanjiao Mountain Scenic Area and the outside world. Driven by its radiation, characteristic industries develop well. It's worthy the name of the people's well-being road, the tourism road, and the wealth creation road.

湖北省恩施土家族苗族自治州恩施市农村公路
Rural Road in Enshi City, Enshi Tujia and Miao Autonomous Prefecture, Hubei Province

湖南省湘西自治州花垣县十八洞村最美通村公路
The Most Beautiful Access Road to Shibadong Village in Huayuan County, Xiangxi Autonomous Prefecture, Hunan Province

"Top 10 Most Beautiful Rural Roads" in 2021

地处武陵山腹地的花垣县十八洞村，曾是交通闭塞、极度贫困的深山苗寨，进村路是 3 米宽的土路。如今，公路打通了，车辆进村了，游客进寨了，产业发展了，年轻人"飞"回村庄了，农业特色产品运出去了，沿线群众的腰包逐渐鼓起来了。

Located in the hinterland of the Wuling Mountains, Shibadong village in Huayuan county was once a Miao village with closed transportation and extreme poverty, and the road leading to the village was a 3-meter wind dirt road. Nowadays, a rural road has been built. Vehicles and tourists went into the village, industries developed, young people came back, agricultural specialty products shipped out, people living along the road are getting richer and richer.

广东省河源市龙川县龙川 1 号公路
Longchuan No.1 Rural Road in Longchuan County, Heyuan City, Guangdong Province

广西壮族自治区柳州市柳江区渡村至成团公路
Ducun-Chengtuan Road in Liujiang District,
Liuzhou City, Guangxi Zhuang Autonomous Region

2021年"十大最美农村路"

"Top 10 Most Beautiful Rural Roads" in 2021

柳江区渡村至成团公路的建成不仅切实提高了红色旅游景点的通达水平，扩大了对外影响力，吸引了大批游客前往参观，还将红色旅游与农业旅游联通起来，形成联动效应，助力乡村振兴建设。

The completion of the road from Ducun to Chengtuan in Liujiang district has not only effectively improved the accessibility of red tourism sites, expanded external influence and attracted a large number of tourists, but also linked red tourism with agro-tourism and help rural revitalization construction.

WEALTH CREATION ROAD 致 富 路

广西壮族自治区桂林市农村公路
Rural Road in Guilin City, Guangxi Zhuang Autonomous Region

海南省五指山市牙胡梯田农村公路
Yahu Terraced Rural Road in Wuzhishan City, Hainan Province

中国"四好农村路" RURAL ROADS IN CHINA

WEALTH CREATION ROAD 致 富 路

"十大最美农村路"

"Top 10 Most Beautiful Rural Roads" in 2022

　　原下庄天路是一条 2～3 米宽的泥结碎石路段，常年晴天扬尘、雨天泥泞，当地村民出行困难。如今，该路段升级硬化成了 4.5 米宽的水泥路面，大大改善了当地村民的出行条件，有了对外联系的通道，就有了发展产业、脱贫致富、实现小康的基础。

The original Xiazhuang "Sky Road" was a 2-3 meters wide muddy gravel road, which was dusty on sunny days and muddy on rainy days, making it difficult for local villagers to travel. Nowadays, this road has been upgraded and hardened into a 4.5-meter wide cement road, greatly improving the travel conditions for local villagers.

重庆市巫山县竹贤乡下庄天路
Xiazhuang "Sky Road" in Zhuxian Township, Wushan County, Chongqing Municipality

四川省凉山州布拖县阿布洛哈村通村公路
Access Road to Abuluoha Village in Butuo County, Liangshan Prefecture, Sichuan Province

"阿布洛哈"在彝语中意为"高山中的深谷""人迹罕至的地方"。阿布洛哈村毗邻金沙江大峡谷，三面环山、一面临崖，群山阻隔、交通闭塞。通村公路全线贯通，连接了乡村与城市，打通了贫瘠与富足、困顿与希望。

"Abuluoha" means "a deep valley in the mountains" and "a place rarely visited by humans" in the Yi language. Abuluoha village is located near the Grand Canyon of the Jinsha River, with mountains surrounding it on three sides and a cliff facing the other. The mountains blocked the way, making transportation difficult. The access road to the village was fully completed, connecting the countryside with the city, bridging the gap between poverty and prosperity, as well as between hardship and hope.

2020年"十大最美农村路"
"Top 10 Most Beautiful Rural Roads" in 2020

四川省凉山彝族自治州农村公路
Rural Road in Liangshan Yi Autonomous Prefecture, Sichuan Province

贵州省遵义市湄潭 27°茶海路
27°Chahai Road in Meitan County, Zunyi City, Guizhou Province

"Top 10 Most Beautiful Rural Roads" in 2020

茶海路因需施景，打造特色生态廊道，遵循"嘉者收之、俗者屏之、乱者统之"的打造思路，最大程度呈现茶田风光的自然美、生态美。在通达便利、服务完善、体验丰富的交通通行条件下，基本实现"茶区变景区，茶园变公园，茶山变金山"，村民"人人是股东，户户能分红，年年有收益"。

Chahai Road creates a unique ecological corridor which reveals the natural and ecological beauty of the tea fields to the fullest extent.

WEALTH CREATION ROAD 致 富 路

云南省曲靖市马龙区农村公路
Rural Road in Malong District, Qujing City, Yunnan Province

西藏自治区昌都市边坝县农村公路
Rural Road in Bianba County, Changdu City, Xizang Autonomous Region

WEALTH CREATION ROAD 致 富 路

陕西省安康市白河县界岭盘山公路

Jieling Mountain Road in Baihe County, Ankang City, Shaanxi Province

中国"四好农村路" RURAL ROADS IN CHINA

陕西省汉中市佛坪县两大路（两河口至大坪峪风景区）
Liangda Road (from Lianghekou to Dapingyu Scenic Area) in Foping County, Hanzhong City, Shaanxi Province

两河口至大坪峪风景区公路方便了公路沿线群众的出行，促进了地方旅游业的蓬勃发展，实现了自然风光与人文资源、绿色文化与乡村文化的有机结合，成功地将乡村旅游、农旅融合、扶贫开发等多个方面相连，为乡村振兴和新业态发展提供了有力支撑。

Liangda Road has facilitated the travel of people along the route, promoted the vigorous development of local tourism, and formed an organic combination of natural scenery and human resources, green culture and rural culture. It has provided a strong support for rural revitalization and the development of new industries.

WEALTH CREATION ROAD 致富路

甘肃省天水市清水县 X307 线农村公路
X307 Rural Road in Qingshui County, Tianshui City, Gansu Province

2020年"十大最美农村路"
"Top 10 Most Beautiful Rural Roads" in 2020

　　X307 线农村公路是"公路、自然、人文"和谐统一的美丽乡村公路示范工程，实现了农村公路与农村经济的有机循环，给当地百姓带来了实实在在的获得感和幸福感。

X307 rural road is a demonstration project which has brought real sense of gain and happiness to local people.

中国"四好农村路" RURAL ROADS IN CHINA

青海省海南藏族自治州共和县农村公路
Rural Road in Gonghe County, Hainan Tibetan Autonomous Prefecture, Qinghai Province

宁夏回族自治区中卫市沙坡头区黄河湾沙漠公路
Desert Road at the Yellow River Bay, Shapotou District, Zhongwei City, Ningxia Hui Autonomous Region

WEALTH CREATION ROAD　致 富 路

新疆维吾尔自治区巴州和静县哈尔莫敦镇至莫西干达坂道路
Road from Halmadun Town to Moxigandaban, Hejing County, Bayingolin Mongolian Autonomous Prefecture, Xinjiang Uygur Autonomous Region

哈尔莫敦镇至莫西干达坂道路穿越崇山峻岭，沿途风光旖旎、景色优美。它的建成加快了沿线水电站、菱镁矿产、特色旅游等资源的开发利用，有效提高了当地牧民的收入，向外界展示了当地的民族特色文化。此路是和静县"扶贫路""小康路""产业路"与"旅游路"的典范。

The road from Halmadun town to Moxigandaban passes through high mountains and embraces beautiful scenery. Its completion has effectively increased the income of local herdsmen, and demonstrated the local characteristic culture to the outside world.

2020年"十大最美农村路"
"Top 10 Most Beautiful Rural Roads" in 2020

中国
"四好农村路"
RURAL ROADS IN
CHINA

幸福路

HAPPINESS ROAD

中国"四好农村路" RURAL ROADS IN CHINA

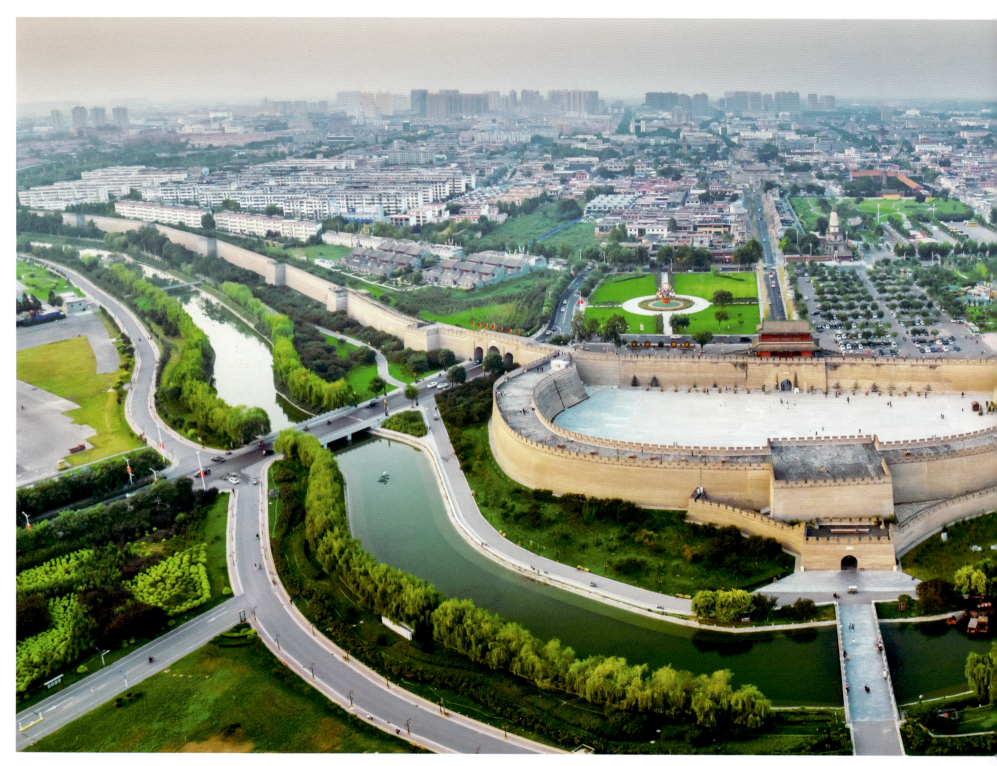

河北省石家庄市正定县农村公路
Rural Road in Zhengding County, Shijiazhuang City, Hebei Province

正定县加快实施"四好农村路"建设，推动"农村公路＋都市农业＋古城文化＋乡村旅游＋康养服务"融合发展，打通了乡村振兴、农民致富的快捷通道。

Zhengding county has accelerated the construction, management, maintenance and operation of rural roads, opening up a fast channel for rural revitalization and farmers' prosperity.

北京市延庆区松闫路
Songyan Road in Yanqing District, Beijing Municipality

2022年"十大最美农村路"

"Top 10 Most Beautiful Rural Roads" in 2022

松闫路作为北京冬奥会延庆赛区关键联络线，展现了科技冬奥魅力。通过安装弯道预警、冰雪预警及行人安全系统，精准应对急弯、暗冰等挑战，以科技赋能提升道路安全性与通行效率。

Songyan Road, as the key contact line of the Yanqing competition area of Beijing Winter Olympic Games, shows the charm of science and technology of Winter Olympic Games. Through the installation of curve warning, ice and snow warning and pedestrian safety system, the road accurately responds to challenges such as sharp curves and dark ice, and enhances road safety and traffic efficiency with technological measures.

天津市蓟州区农村公路
Rural Road in Jizhou District, Tianjin Municipality

河北省承德市围场满族蒙古族自治县农村公路

Rural Road in Weichang Manchu and Mongolian Autonomous County, Chengde City, Hebei Province

河北省邯郸市峰峰矿区 0 号旅游路

No. 0 Tourism Road in Fengfeng Mining Area, Handan City, Hebei Province

中国"四好农村路" RURAL ROADS IN CHINA

山西省临汾市永和县黄河一号旅游公路南庄—阁底段

Nanzhuang to Gedi Section of the Yellow River No.1 Tourism Road in Yonghe County, Linfen City, Shanxi Province

"Top 10 Most Beautiful Rural Roads" in 2020

黄河一号旅游公路南庄—阁底段孕育于红色文化中，开辟于青山绿水间，蜿蜒于蓝天白云下。空中俯瞰，如蛟龙盘踞，气势恢宏，又如玉带环绕，百转千回。景色之美、风物之魅和人文之韵，使这条旅游公路集最美风景、绿色生态为一体。

The section from Nanzhuang to Gedi of the Yellow River No.1 tourism road is bred in the red culture, integrating beautiful scenery and green ecology.

山西省运城市沿黄旅游公路
Tourism Road along the Yellow River in Yuncheng City, Shanxi Province

内蒙古自治区鄂尔多斯市杭锦旗穿沙公路
Desert Road in Hangjin Banner, Ordos City, Inner Mongolia Autonomous Region

鄂尔多斯市杭锦旗位于库布其沙漠腹地，穿沙公路纵贯杭锦旗南北。伴随杭锦旗路网的逐步完善，林沙产业兴了、光伏生态电站来了、沙漠特色旅游活了，"沙进人退"转变为"路进沙退"，展现了杭锦旗公路畅、生态美、百姓富的巨大变化。

The desert road runs north-south through Hangjin Banner. The gradual improvement of the road network in Hangjin Banner has demonstrated significant changes in the area, including smooth road, beautiful ecology, and prosperity of the people.

内蒙古自治区呼伦贝尔市额尔古纳市额尔古纳湿地公路
Erguna Wetland Road in Erguna City, Hulunbuir City, Inner Mongolia Autonomous Region

辽宁省大连市金普新区金七线
Jinqi Road in Jinpu New Area, Dalian City, Liaoning Province

吉林省松原市前郭尔罗斯蒙古族自治县查干湖安代路
Andai Road to Chagan Lake in Qianguorosi Mongol Autonomous County, Songyuan City, Jilin Province

2021年"我家门口那条路——最具人气的路"
"The Road in Front of My House —The Most Popular Road" in 2021

黑龙江省佳木斯市汤原县汤亮公路
Tangliang Road in Tangyuan County, Jiamusi City, Heilongjiang Province

汤亮公路与大自然森林氧吧高度契合，沿线秀美风光与美丽的农村公路相互结合，促进了交通＋扶贫、交通＋旅游的深度融合，已成为汤原县"四好农村路"高质量发展的示范路、全域旅游和美丽乡村建设中的靓丽风景线。

Tangliang Road is highly compatible with forest and combines with beautiful scenery along the route. It promotes deep integration of transportation and poverty alleviation as well as transportation and tourism. It has become a demonstration road for the high-quality development of the construction, management, maintenance and operation of rural roads in Tangyuan county, as well as a beautiful scenic spot in the construction of whole-area tourism and beautiful countryside.

上海市奉贤区树桓路

Shuhuan Road in Fengxian District, Shanghai Municipality

上海市嘉定区徐行镇伏弄路

Funong Road in Xuhang Town, Jiading District, Shanghai Municipality

江苏省盐城市东台市旅游公路1号线东台段

Dongtai Section of No.1 Tourism Road in Dongtai City, Yancheng City, Jiangsu Province

东台市旅游公路1号线东台段以"蓝色海港浪漫之路"为主题,串联起国家级中小城镇生态实验区弶港镇、黄海国家森林公园、世界遗产名录条子泥、全国生态文化村巴斗村,沿线大批具有地方特色的产业相继落户道路周边区域,进一步带动了地方农村经济的快速发展。

The Dongtai section of No.1 tourism road in Dongtai city strings up the beautiful countryside, and also makes a large number of industries with local characteristics settled in the area around the road, further driving the rapid development of local rural economy.

江苏省苏州市东山太湖景观公路
Scenic Road around Dongshan Taihu Lake in Suzhou City, Jiangsu Province

2022年
"十大最美农村路"

"Top 10 Most Beautiful Rural Roads" in 2022

环太湖公路是国内首条省际合作建设的风景路，也是长三角区域一体化发展的实践载体；不仅是联通两省四市的交通道路，更是一条串联两省四市文旅党建、智慧创新、农民致富、乡村振兴的"大动脉"，是农村公路建设的"太湖样板"。它带领沿线百姓走上了生态宜居、便捷出行、大幅增收的幸福大道，成为跳跃在太湖南岸的一串动人音符。

The road around Taihu Lake is the first scenic road built by inter-provincial cooperation in China, and is also a practical carrier of the integrated development of the Yangtze River Delta region. It has led the people along the route to embark on a path of ecological livability, convenient travel, and substantial income growth.

江浙两省四市（苏州市、湖州市、无锡市、常州市）环太湖公路
Road around Taihu Lake in Suzhou, Huzhou, Wuxi and Changzhou City, Jiangsu and Zhejiang Province

中国"四好农村路" RURAL ROADS IN CHINA

浙江省金华市婺城区盘山公路

Mountain Road in Wucheng District, Jinhua City, Zhejiang Province

2023年 "我家门口那条路——最具人气的路"

"The Road in Front of My House —The Most Popular Road" in 2023

浙江省台州市仙居县环神仙居旅游公路
Tourism Road around Shenxianju in Xianju County, Taizhou City, Zhejiang Province

环神仙居旅游公路全线蓝天流云，空谷幽兰，满目苍翠，山水相间，美景无边。白居易笔下《忆江南》中所描写的"春来江水绿如蓝"，可以在沿线的浅溪中复现，有"车在路上走，人在画中游"的体验。公路串起沿线众多农家乐、民宿村，带动美丽经济蓬勃发展，把公路打造成乡村振兴和农民致富加速带，让绿水青山变成金山银山。

The tourism road around Shenxianju strings up many agritainment resorts and lodging villages along the route, driving the prosperous development of economy, and turning the clear waters and green mountains into invaluable assets.

安徽省安庆市岳西县农村公路
Rural Road in Yuexi County, Anqing City, Anhui Province

福建省福州市平潭县平潭岛环岛公路

Road around Pingtan Island in Pingtan County, Fuzhou City, Fujian Province

"Top 10 Most Beautiful Rural Roads" in 2019

福建省福州市晋安北峰环线全景公路鼓宦线
Guhuan Line of Beifeng Ring Road in Jin'an District, Fuzhou City, Fujian Province

　　北峰环线全景公路鼓宦线是一条"观景之路",行驶其上,路边的福州城区美景尽收眼底;是一条"色彩之路",在不同的季节,都有别样的风景;是一条"振兴之路",通往鼓岭国家级旅游度假区,带动鼓岭旅游迎来新发展。

The Guhuan line of Beifeng ring road is a "scenic road", with extraordinary landscape of Fuzhou city on both sides. It is a "colorful road", with different scenery in different seasons, as well as a "revitalization road", bringing new development to the tourism in Guling.

HAPPINESS ROAD 幸 福 路

江西省赣州市于都县农村公路

Rural Road in Yudu County, Ganzhou City, Jiangxi Province

江西省上饶市婺源县江岭风景区公路
Road in Jiangling Scenic Area,
Shangrao City, Jiangxi Province

最美乡村婺源，一条条农村公路别具特色，风景宜人。公路沿线串起了江岭花海、篁岭晒秋、思溪延村明清古建筑群等自然风光和人文景观。

The rural road in Wuyuan embraces unique and pleasant scenery. It strings up natural scenery and human landscape.

山东省临沂市蒙阴县农村公路
Rural Road in Mengyin County, Linyi City, Shandong Province

山东省潍坊市安丘市"天路"（十徐路）
Shixu Road in Anqiu City, Weifang City, Shandong Province

十徐路是安丘旅游公路的一部分，它像一条巨龙，盘旋在群山间，因所处偏远，地势高险，蜿蜒曲折，修筑难度大，被誉为安丘"天路"。它将7个特色小镇、30个休闲农庄和一批精品农家乐串点成线、串珠成链，打造了红色游、文化游、生态游、休闲游等8条精品旅游线路，带活了乡村旅游发展。

Shixu Road is part of the Anqiu tourism road. It is known as Anqiu "sky road". It strings up 7 characteristic towns, 30 leisure farms and a number of agritainment resorts. 8 boutique tourism routes were launched. Rural tourism develops vigorously.

河南省开封市兰考县兰赵线
Lanzhao Road in Lankao County, Kaifeng City, Henan Province

"Top 10 Most Beautiful Rural Roads" in 2021

兰赵线围绕"交通+"模式，以路即是景，修一条路、造一片景、富一方百姓为理念，不仅串联起兰考乡村风景线，更为企业入驻、种植产业发展提供了便利的交通条件。

Lanzhao Road not only connects the rural scenic spots in Lankao, but also provides convenient transportation conditions for the enterprises to settle in and for the development of planting industry.

湖北省宜昌市远安县花百路

Huabai Road in Yuan'an County, Yichang City, Hubei Province

广东省惠州市博罗县罗浮1号公路

Luofu No.1 Road in Boluo County, Huizhou City, Guangdong Province

中国"四好农村路"　RURAL ROADS IN CHINA

广西壮族自治区柳州市鹿寨县农村公路

Rural Road in Luzhai County, Liuzhou City, Guangxi Zhuang Autonomous Region

海南省万宁市日月湾旅游公路

Tourism Road at Riyue Bay in Wanning City, Hainan Province

海南省文昌市木兰湾农村公路
Rural Road at Mulan Bay, Wenchang City, Hainan Province

湖南省长沙市长沙县青山铺—开慧红色旅游专线
Qingshanpu-Kaihui Red Tourism Road in Changsha County, Changsha City, Hunan Province

青山铺—开慧红色旅游专线是长沙县内重要的纵向连接线，既承担了沿线乡镇百姓生产生活的集疏运功能，又串联了天华纪念馆、影珠山抗战遗址、陈树湘故居、开慧纪念馆等红色景点。

Qingshanpu-Kaihui red tourism road is an important longitudinal connection in Changsha county, which not only undertakes the collection and transportation functions for the production and life of the people in the townships along the route, but also connects the red tourism attractions.

2023年"十大最美农村路"

"Top 10 Most Beautiful Rural Roads" in 2023

中国"四好农村路"　RURAL ROADS IN CHINA

重庆市涪陵区白武路

Baiwu Road in Fuling District, Chongqing Municipality

"Top 10 Most Beautiful Rural Roads" in 2021

　　白武路是一条依山而建，盘山向上的"Z"形山区农村公路，沿途山峰、台地、沟谷高低错落，层次丰富，山势奇峻多姿，极具壮观之美。它将生态建设、全域旅游、文化传承、乡村振兴等内容有机结合，是一条武陵山区百姓通往城区的幸福路。

Baiwu Road is a "Z" shaped rural road built in the mountainous area. It combines ecological construction, whole-area tourism, cultural heritage and rural revitalization, leading people in the Wuling Mountain area to the urban area.

四川省阿坝藏族羌族自治州小金县四姑娘山海子沟公路
Haizigou Road of Siguniang Mountain in Xiaojin County,
Aba Tibetan and Qiang Autonomous Prefecture, Sichuan Province

四川省巴中市平昌县板青路
Banqing Road in Pingchang County, Bazhong City, Sichuan Province

2019年"十大最美农村路"
"Top 10 Most Beautiful Rural Roads" in 2019

　　板青路的辐射带动，使板庙、青凤、石垭、鹿鸣等乡镇农村公路融合成网、互联互通，一举改变了曾经落后的生产生活面貌，沿线建成大石村现代农业产业园、白石村桃花谷等。板青路已真正成为重塑乡村魅力、传递乡风文明、留住乡愁乡味的重要载体。

The radiation drive of Banqing Road has integrated the rural roads in townships into a network with interconnection, and has changed the production and living conditions. Banqing Road has truly become an important carrier for reshaping the charm and transmitting the civilization of the countryside.

贵州省黔东南苗族侗族自治州月亮山农村公路
Rural Road of Yueliang Mountain in Qiandongnan Miao and Dong Autonomous Prefecture, Guizhou Province

2021年
"我家门口那条路
——最具人气的路"

"The Road in Front of My House
—The Most Popular Road" in 2021

云南省昆明市宜良县 68 道拐公路
Road with 68 Turns in Yiliang County, Kunming City, Yunnan Province

68 道拐公路依山梁而修，因全线共有 68 道拐而得名。它连接了靖安哨与小白龙森林公园，是一条集自然风光、历史文化于一体的生态旅游路线，让游客在体验驾驶乐趣的同时，领略岩泉古韵与彝家风情，成为自驾游爱好者的必驾之路。

The road with 68 turns connects Jing'anshao and Xiaobailong Forest Park. It is an eco-tourism route which integrates natural scenery and historical culture, allowing tourists to experience the joy of driving while enjoying the ancient charm of Yanquan and the ethnic customs of the Yi people.

西藏自治区林芝市波密县桃花沟景区公路
Road in Taohuagou Scenic Area, Bomi County, Linzhi City, Xizang Autonomous Region

陕西省宝鸡市陈仓区九龙山旅游公路

Jiulongshan Tourism Road in Chencang District, Baoji City, Shaanxi Province

九龙山旅游公路融入"公路＋旅游"理念，保护自然风貌，打造多样景观，配套完善服务设施，实现了路景相融，不仅推动了旅游业的繁荣，更带动了周边群众就业创业，让绿水青山成为群众增收致富的金山银山。

The design of Jiulongshan tourism road incorporates the concept of "highway + tourism" to protect the natural appearance, create diverse landscape, and improve service facilities. It not only promotes the prosperity of the tourism industry but also drives employment and entrepreneurship among the surrounding people, turning clear waters and green mountains into invaluable assets.

陕西省西安市周至县周塬路

Zhouyuan Road in Zhouzhi County, Xi'an City, Shaanxi Province

甘肃省临夏回族自治州东乡族自治县折红公路

Zhehong Road in Dongxiang Autonomous County, Linxia Hui Autonomous Prefecture, Gansu Province

HAPPINESS ROAD 〜 幸 福 路

青海省海南藏族自治州贵德县拉脊山农村公路

Rural Road of Laji Mountain in Guide County, Hainan Tibetan Autonomous Prefecture, Qinghai Province

宁夏回族自治区中卫市沙坡头区 66 号公路
No.66 Road in Shapotou District, Zhongwei City, Ningxia Hui Autonomous Region

新疆维吾尔自治区阿克苏地区温宿县托峰天路（G314 线 K969+660 岔口—塔格拉克牧场）
Tuofeng "Sky Road" in Wensu County, Aksu Prefecture, Xinjiang Uygur Autonomous Region

"Top 10 Most Beautiful Rural Roads" in 2023

托峰天路（G314 线 K969+660 岔口—塔格拉克牧场）作为乡村振兴的"旅游路"，以其独特的风景成为"沙枣画廊"。改扩建后，显著提升了道路通行条件，助力塔格拉克村乡村旅游蓬勃发展，"归园田居·塔村"品牌名声大噪，成为温宿县旅游新亮点。

Tuofeng "Sky Road" is a tourism road for rural revitalization with unique scenery. After the reconstruction and expansion, it significantly improves the road access conditions, and helps the rural tourism of Tagrak village to develop vigorously.

新疆维吾尔自治区昌吉回族自治州奇台县农村公路
Rural Road in Qitai County, Changji Hui Autonomous Prefecture, Xinjiang Uygur Autonomous Region

中国
"四好农村路"
RURAL ROADS IN
CHINA

连心路

HEART CONNECTION ROAD

中国"四好农村路" RURAL ROADS IN CHINA

曾经"车岭车上天,九岭爬九年"的下党乡,如今已经建成5条进乡公路、10条通村公路,实现了"天堑变通途"的华丽转身。农村公路带动了乡村经济的发展,让下党乡有了通往幸福的康庄大道,走出一条具有闽东特色的乡村振兴之路。

5 township roads and 10 village roads have been built in Xiadang township. Rural roads drive the development of rural economy, so that Xiadang township has opened up a broad road to happiness, and found a rural revitalization road with the characteristics of eastern Fujian.

福建省宁德市寿宁县下党乡农村公路
Rural Road in Xiadang Township, Shouning County, Ningde City, Fujian Province

HEART CONNECTION ROAD 连 心 路

北京市怀柔区喇叭沟门满族乡农村公路

Rural Road in Labagoumen Manchu Township, Huairou District, Beijing Municipality

中国"四好农村路" RURAL ROADS IN CHINA

河北省石家庄市平山县西柏坡农村公路
Rural Road in Xibaipo Village, Pingshan County, Shijiazhuang City, Hebei Province

西柏坡村水碧山青，云雾霭霭，水光山色之间，美丽乡村错落有致，宛如一幅幅山水画徐徐展开。西柏坡农村公路让崎岖山路变坦途，让乡亲们"出门水泥路、抬脚就上车、家门收快递"梦想成为现实，让旅游者纷至沓来、流连忘返，是一条"传承西柏坡精神、讲好西柏坡的故事"的幸福路。

Xibaipo village is surrounded by clean waters and green mountains, with misty clouds hovering over it. The rural road has attracted numerous tourists. It is a happiness road which "carries on the spirit of Xibaipo and tells the story of Xibaipo".

中国"四好农村路" RURAL ROADS IN CHINA

河北省邢台市信都区抗大路
Kangda Road in Xindu District, Xingtai City, Hebei Province

八百里巍巍太行，钟灵毓秀在信都。抗大路是在太行之脊修筑出的一条天路，全长48公里。驱车行驶其上，处处可见红色元素。旧址村彼此互通、串珠成链。抗大陈列馆108级台阶拾级而上。如今，这些被岁月浸润过的红色记忆，正静静地见证革命"红色"与太行"绿色"之间一直交相辉映的抗大精神。

Kangda Road is built on the ridge of Taihang Mountains, with a total length of 48 kilometers. Driving on it, red elements can be seen everywhere. The old villages are interconnected with each other, forming a chain of pearls.

2022年"十大最美农村路"
"Top 10 Most Beautiful Rural Roads" in 2022

HEART CONNECTION ROAD 连 心 路

山西省太原市西山"一线天"旅游公路
"Yixiantian" Tourism Road in Xishan, Taiyuan City, Shanxi Province

山西省运城市河津市沿黄旅游公路（乡宁至西范段）
Tourism Road along the Yellow River (Xiangning-Xifan Section) in Hejin City, Yuncheng City, Shanxi Province

河津市沿黄旅游公路（乡宁至西范段）遵循"濒临黄河、亲近自然"的设计思路，路线全部沿黄河东岸布设，开启了河津交通史上旅游公路专线专用的先河，为河津市全域旅游发展提供了强有力的交通支撑，也为沿线农业的发展打通了销售通道，更辐射带动了周边群众走上农业种植的致富路。

The tourism road along the Yellow River (Xiangning-Xifan Section) in Hejin city follows the design concept of "adjacent to the Yellow River, close to the nature". It has provided a strong transportation support for the development of whole-area tourism in Hejin city, opened up the sales channel for the agriculture development along the route, and driven the surrounding people to become richer and richer through agricultural cultivation.

内蒙古自治区锡林郭勒盟西乌珠穆沁旗草原"99号公路"
No. 99 Road on the Grassland of West Ujimqin Banner, Xilin Gol League, Inner Mongolia Autonomous Region

辽宁省沈阳市沈北新区农村公路
Rural Road in Shenbei New Area, Shenyang City, Liaoning Province

2020年 "十大最美农村路"
"Top 10 Most Beautiful Rural Roads" in 2020

吉林省长春市双阳区神鹿峰旅游公路
Shenlufeng Tourism Road in Shuangyang District, Changchun City, Jilin Province

黑龙江省大兴安岭地区漠河市北极村农村公路

Rural Road in Beiji Village, Mohe City, Daxing'anling Prefecture, Heilongjiang Province

上海市金山区朱泾镇待泾村蒋泾中心路
Jiangjing Central Road in Daijing Village, Zhujing Town, Jinshan District, Shanghai Municipality

上海市青浦区金泽镇紫莲路
Zilian Road in Jinze Town, Qingpu District, Shanghai Municipality

紫莲路，独具"莲湖水韵·归田园居"的典型江南水乡特色，是自然环境和古镇人文高度融合的生态旅游路，成为建设长三角生态绿色一体化发展示范区"水乡客厅"的典型缩影。

Zilian Road is an eco-tourism road where the natural environment and the ancient town's cultural heritage are highly integrated. It serves as a typical microcosm in the construction of the Yangtze River Delta Ecological Green Integrated Development Demonstration Zone.

江苏省常州市溧阳市溧阳1号公路瓦屋山线
Wawu Mountain Line of Liyang No.1 Road in Liyang City, Changzhou City, Jiangsu Province

"Top 10 Most Beautiful Rural Roads" in 2019

溧阳1号公路，是江苏省首批旅游风景道，也是全国美丽乡村公路和全国十大最美农村公路之一。以路为引，串点引线，勾勒溧阳最美的山水，留存游子记忆的原乡，彰显千年古邑的悠久，感受溧阳城市的情怀。这条路不仅成为溧阳80万老百姓的幸福路、致富路，更打通了"绿水青山"与"金山银山"之间的通道。

Liyang No.1 Road is one of the first batch of tourism scenic roads in Jiangsu province, and also is one of the national beautiful rural roads and the top ten most beautiful rural roads in China. It outlines the most beautiful landscape of Liyang, and shows the longevity of the thousand-year old city. This road has not only become the happiness road and wealth creation road for 800,000 people in Liyang, but also opened up the channel between "clear waters and green mountains" and "invaluable assets".

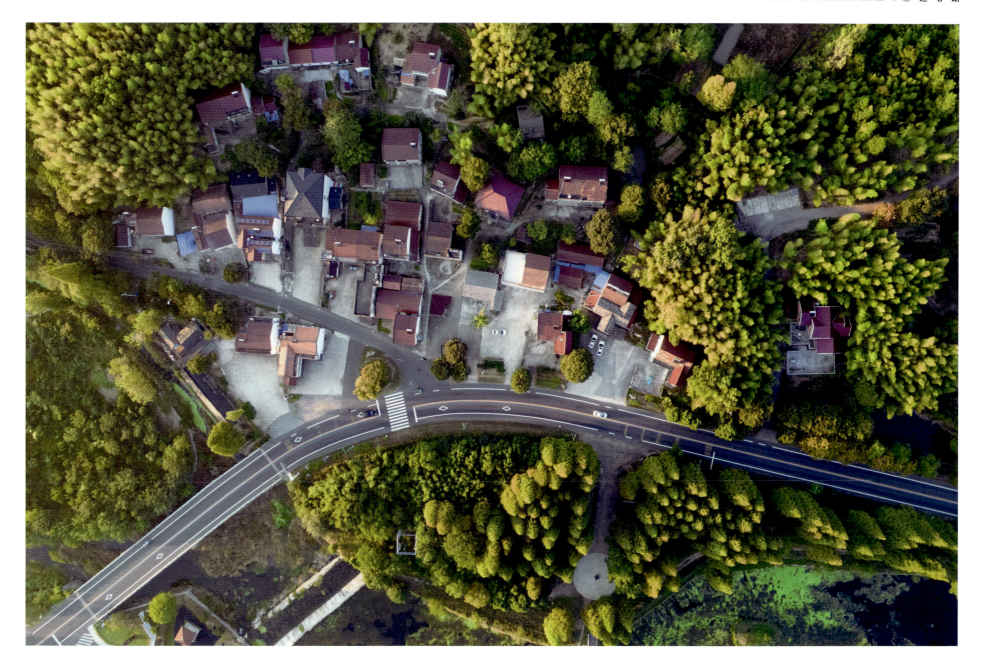

江苏省常州市溧阳市白六干村农村公路

Rural Road in Bailiugan Village, Liyang City, Changzhou City, Jiangsu Province

中国"四好农村路" RURAL ROADS IN CHINA

HEART CONNECTION ROAD　连 心 路

"Top 10 Most Beautiful Rural Roads" in 2021

浙江省嘉兴市南湖区七沈公路
Qishen Road in Nanhu District, Jiaxing City, Zhejiang Province

　　七沈公路地处"初心之地"——浙江省嘉兴市，突出展现了"精神传承、使命永恒"的主题，形成了一条"点上有故事、面上有风景、线上有体验"的精品红色旅游示范线，成为红船起航地的一张亮丽新名片。

Qishen Road is a boutique red tourism demonstration route, and has become a bright new name card of Jiaxing city.

中国"四好农村路" RURAL ROADS IN CHINA

浙江省宁波市余姚市梁弄镇横坎头村农村公路

Rural Road in Hengkantou Village, Liangnong Town, Yuyao City, Ningbo City, Zhejiang Province

"The Road in Front of My House
—The Most Popular Road" in 2022

安徽省池州市贵池区黄栗路
Huangli Road in Guichi District, Chizhou City, Anhui Province

  黄栗路是一条集交通、文旅、产业发展于一体的农村公路，也是一条自然和美、顺达通畅的乡风文明路。它畅通了农家乐与山水鉴赏相结合的绿色经济"毛细血管"，让农区变景区、农房变客房、田园变乐园，串起了一道道乡村致富的风景线。

Huangli Road is a rural road which integrates transportation, cultural tourism, and industry development. It is also a civilized rural road with natural beauty and smooth traffic. It has strung up a series of beautiful landscape for rural prosperity.

福建省平潭综合实验区北部生态廊道 Y049
Y049 Northern Ecological Corridor in Pingtan Comprehensive Experimental Zone, Fujian Province

"The Road in Front of My House
—The Most Popular Road" in 2020

　　北部生态廊道 Y049 聚焦"原生态 + 现代化",路线设计依山就势,避开沿线生态脆弱敏感点,在充分保护原生植被的基础上,采用抗候及适应能力较好的绿植,通过科学修复工艺实现工程建设与生态保护并重。运用"现代化改造 + 文化植入"方式,精心打造沿线观景平台。建成开放后,吸引众多游客慕名前来,助力平潭北部旅游驶上"快车道"。

Y049 northern ecological corridor focuses on "original ecology and modernization". The route design follows the mountains and avoids the ecologically fragile and sensitive points along the routes. Based on the full protection of native vegetation, green plants with good climate resistance and adaptability are used, and scientific restoration technologies are adopted to achieve the balance between engineering construction and ecological protection. It attracts many tourists and helps the tourism in the northern part of Pingtan to develop vigorously.

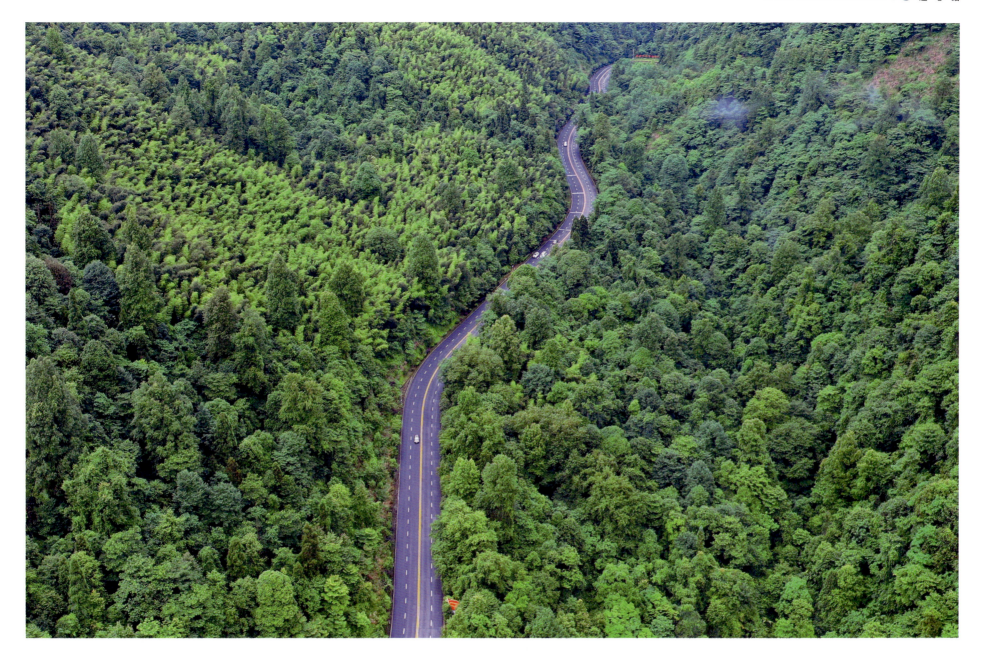

传承红色基因、赓续红色血脉。井冈山市依托丰富的旅游资源,通过农村路网建设,把革命旧址遗迹、红色名村、自然风光等串珠成线、连线成面,实现了交通运输与旅游的融合发展。

Relying on rich tourism resources, Jinggangshan city realized the integrated development of transportation and tourism through the construction of rural road network.

江西省吉安市井冈山市农村公路

Rural Road in Jinggangshan City, Ji'an City, Jiangxi Province

中国"四好农村路" RURAL ROADS IN CHINA

山东省枣庄市山亭区环岩马湖农村公路
Road around Yanma Lake in Shanting District, Zaozhuang City, Shandong Province

HEART CONNECTION ROAD 连 心 路

山东省临沂市"爱尚沂南 红色之旅"环线
Ring Road in Linyi City, Shandong Province

"Top 10 Most Beautiful Rural Roads" in 2020

"爱尚沂南 红色之旅"环线是沂南县红嫂纪念馆到孟良崮战役纪念馆的一条"红色专线"。它将沂南县红色教育基地与孟良崮纪念馆连成一线,加快了全域旅游发展,助推了现代农业发展,带动了城乡客运服务,促进了农村物流业发展。

The ring road connects the red education bases in Yinan county and Menglianggu Battle Monument. It accelerates the development of regional tourism, promotes the development of modern agriculture, and spurs the development of urban and rural passenger transportation services as well as rural logistics.

中国"四好农村路" RURAL ROADS IN CHINA

河南省安阳市林州市林石公路

Linshi Road in Linzhou City, Anyang City, Henan Province

"Top 10 Most Beautiful Rural Roads" in 2019

　　林石公路是连接太行大峡谷5A级景区的重要旅游通道，一头连着充满活力的城市，一头连着太行深处的村庄。它将喧嚣与静谧、现代与古朴紧密连接在一起，成为安阳市、河南省和全国的"最美农村公路"，真正实现了"修一条路、造一片景、富一方民"。

Linshi Road is an important tourism channel connecting the Taihang Grand Canyon. It has become one of the "Most Beautiful Rural Roads" in Anyang city, Henan province and even the whole country.

湖北省黄冈市红安县经典旅游景区公路
Road in Classic Tourism Scenic Area, Hong'an County, Huanggang City, Hubei Province

红安县经典旅游景区公路是一条传播红色文化、带动红色旅游品质提升、助力绿色生态产业腾飞的红色之旅初心路。

The road in classic tourism scenic area of Hong'an county is a red tourism road which spreads the red culture, improves the quality of red tourism, and helps the green ecological industry to develop vigorously.

2022年 "我家门口那条路——最具人气的路"
"The Road in Front of My House—The Most Popular Road" in 2022

湖南省怀化市通道侗族自治县生态游廊

Ecological Corridor in Tongdao Dong Autonomous County, Huaihua City, Hunan Province

广东省江门市开平市邑美侨路

Yimeiqiao Road in Kaiping City, Jiangmen City, Guangdong Province

中国"四好农村路" RURAL ROADS IN CHINA

广西壮族自治区梧州市岑溪市农村公路
Rural Road in Cenxi City, Wuzhou City, Guangxi Zhuang Autonomous Region

海南省昌江黎族自治县农村公路
Rural Road in Changjiang Li Autonomous County, Hainan Province

"Top 10 Most Beautiful Rural Roads" in 2020

重庆市梁平区渔米路
Yumi Road in Liangping District, Chongqing Municipality

渔米路因串联渝东平原的十万亩优质稻田和万亩生态渔园而得名，全长 21.15 公里，是践行新发展理念的产业路、旅游路、样板路。渔米路与国道 243 线、省道 510 线相连，与 G5515 张南高速公路相通，为农产品进入梁平工业园区深加工及对外运输提供了快速通道。

Yumi Road is named after its connection of high-quality rice fields and ecological fishing parks in the Yudong Plain. The road is 21.15 kilometers long, and is connected with National Highway 243, Provincial Highway 510, and G5515 Zhangnan Expressway, providing a fast channel for agricultural products to enter Liangping Industrial District for deep processing and external transportation.

HEART CONNECTION ROAD 连 心 路

四川省阿坝藏族羌族自治州壤塘县"上南天路"
"Shangnan Sky Road" in Rangtang County, Aba Tibetan and Qiang Autonomous Prefecture, Sichuan Province

"上南天路"蜿蜒前行,打通了牧民出行的"最后一公里",被当地居民亲切地称为高原净土之上"离天堂最近的路"。路通后,牧民们买上了摩托车、汽车,过去"马背牛驮"式的搬运变成汽车运送。对于牧民而言,这更是一条脱贫致富路。

"Shangnan Sky Road" is affectionately called by local residents as the road closest to heaven on the pure land of the plateau. After the opening of the road, herdsmen bought motorcycles and cars, and transportation by cars has been realized. For herdsmen, this is a road to poverty alleviation and wealth creation.

四川省成都市邛崃市平临夹路
Pinglinjia Road in Qionglai City, Chengdu City, Sichuan Province

贵州省遵义市播州区枫元至苟坝红色乡愁路

Rural Road from Fengyuan to Gouba in Bozhou District, Zunyi City, Guizhou Province

"Top 10 Most Beautiful Rural Roads" in 2022

花茂村过去叫"荒茅田",是一个贫困村。近年来,花茂村大力发展"乡愁经济"。枫元至苟坝红色乡愁路串联起沿线枫元村、土坝村、花茂村、苟坝村4村,依托便利交通,当地深度挖掘红色旅游、乡村农耕文化等资源,开发了古法造纸、陶艺制作等10多个体验项目,带动100多户农户吃上了"旅游饭"。

The rural road from Fengyuan to Gouba connects four villages along the route. Relying on convenient transportation, the local people have deeply explored resources such as red tourism and rural farming culture, and developed more than 10 experience projects such as ancient papermaking and pottery making, driving more than 100 farmers to make money from tourism.

云南省怒江傈僳族自治州贡山独龙族怒族自治县农村公路

Rural Road in Gongshan Dulong and Nu Autonomous County, Nujiang Lisu Autonomous Prefecture, Yunnan Province

云南省玉溪市新平彝族傣族自治县螺旋桥

Spiral Bridge in Xinping Yi and Dai Autonomous County, Yuxi City, Yunnan Province

西藏自治区日喀则市江孜县农村公路

Rural Road in Gyangze County, Xigaze City, Xizang Autonomous Region

陕西省渭南市富平县金栗山至张桥镇农村公路（美原镇至杨尧段）

Rural Road from Jinli Mountain to Zhangqiao Town (Meiyuan Town–Yangyao Section) in Fuping County, Weinan City, Shaanxi Province

甘肃省武威市天祝藏族自治县农村公路
Rural Road in Tianzhu Tibetan Autonomous County, Wuwei City, Gansu Province

青海省海北藏族自治州祁连县青羊沟公路
Qingyanggou Road in Qilian County, Haibei Tibetan Autonomous Prefecture, Qinghai Province

宁夏回族自治区固原市隆德县农村公路
Rural Road in Longde County, Guyuan City, Ningxia Hui Autonomous Region

中国"四好农村路"　RURAL ROADS IN CHINA

新疆维吾尔自治区吐鲁番市鄯善县农村公路
Rural Road in Shanshan County, Turpan City, Xinjiang Uygur Autonomous Region

2021年 "十大最美农村路"

"Top 10 Most Beautiful Rural Roads" in 2021

新疆维吾尔自治区阿克苏地区新和县排先拜巴扎乡—塔木托格拉克乡—渭干乡农场道路

Paixianbaibazha Township-Tamtograk Township-Weigan Township Farm Road in Xinhe County, Aksu Prefecture, Xinjiang Uygur Autonomous Region

振兴路
REVITALIZATION ROAD

余村作为"绿水青山就是金山银山"理念诞生地,是当地绿色发展中崛起的典型。余村大道是通往余村的重要道路,也是共同富裕之路的缩影。从砂石路到三级公路,从粗放式养护到精细化养护、高质量管理、高水平运营,余村大道的蝶变之路,是余村发展的缩影。现在的余村大道,一头连着人与自然的和谐,一头连着生态经济,打通了绿水青山转化为金山银山的畅途,成为余村绿色发展的"先行官"。

Yucun village, as the birthplace of the concept of "clear waters and green mountains are invaluable assets", is a typical example of the rise of local green development. Yucun village road is an important road leading to Yucun and epitomizes the road to common prosperity. From the gravel road to the class-3 highway, from rough maintenance to fine maintenance, high-quality management, and high-level operation, the transformation of Yucun village road is a microcosm of the development of Yucun village. The current Yucun village road opens up a smooth path for transforming clear waters and green mountains into invaluable assets, and becomes the frontier of local green development.

浙江省湖州市安吉县天荒坪镇余村大道

Yucun Village Road in Tianhuangping Town, Anji County, Huzhou City, Zhejiang Province

REVITALIZATION ROAD 振兴路

"Top 10 Most Beautiful Rural Roads" in 2021

密云水库南线不仅串联起溪翁庄、穆家峪等乡镇的绝美风光，还融合了鱼街、九松山等旅游资源，展现了山、湖、渔、路的和谐共生。沿途的观景平台、民俗村食宿，让游客在领略自然美景的同时，也能深入体验密云的文化底蕴与乡土风情，使密云水库南线成为乡村振兴与旅游发展的典范之路。

The south route of Miyun reservoir not only connects the stunning scenery of townships, but also integrates tourism resources. The scenic platforms and folk villages along the route allow tourists to not only appreciate the natural beauty, but also deeply experience the rich cultural heritage and local customs of Miyun. It has become a model road for rural revitalization and tourism development.

北京市密云区密云水库南线

South Route of Miyun Reservoir in Miyun District, Beijing Municipality

天津市蓟州区山区公路

Mountain Road in Jizhou District, Tianjin Municipality

河北省邯郸市武安市白云大道（活水—柏草坪）
Baiyun Road (Huoshui-Baicaoping) in Wu'an City, Handan City, Hebei Province

"Top 10 Most Beautiful Rural Roads"
In 2023

　　白云大道打通了白云川和管陶川自古以来的道路瓶颈，为两乡人民铺筑了交流互通的坦途。它全长约22公里，以高标准建设，配备完善的安全与景观设施，极大地缩短了通行时间，为武安市旅游业的繁荣奠定了坚实基础。

Baiyun Road has paved a straight path for the people of Baiyunchuan and Guantaochuan townships to communicate and interoperate. It is about 22 kilometers long, constructed to high standards, and equipped with perfect safety and landscape facilities. It has greatly shortened the passage time, and laid a solid foundation for the prosperity of tourism in Wu'an city.

山西省晋城市陵川县太行一号旅游公路（上上河至玛琅山段）
Taihang No.1 Tourism Road (Shangshanghe-Malangshan Section) in Lingchuan County, Jincheng City, Shanxi Province

太行一号旅游公路通过慢行系统、景观提升，实现路景交融。智慧信息系统的融入，让游客享受"一部手机游太行"的便捷。

Taihang No.1 tourism road realizes a harmonious integration of the road and landscape through the slow-moving traffic system and landscape enhancement. The integration of intelligent information system allows tourists to enjoy the convenience of "travelling on the Taihang Mountains with one cell phone".

2023年"我家门口那条路——最具人气的路"

"The Road in Front of My House —The Most Popular Road" in 2023

乌丹至白音套海生态旅游产业路，作为翁牛特旗"以路治沙"的典范，不仅是一条穿沙沥青路面公路，更是生态治理、文化传播、旅游发展与乡村振兴的多功能纽带，对科尔沁沙漠生态环境治理、地区经济社会发展具有重要意义。

The eco-tourism industry road from Wudan to Baiyintaohai is not only a desert-crossing asphalt pavement road, but also a multi-functional link for ecological governance, cultural dissemination, tourism development and rural revitalization. It is of great significance to the management of the ecological environment of the Horqin Desert and to local economic and social development.

内蒙古自治区赤峰市翁牛特旗乌丹至白音套海生态旅游产业路
Eco-tourism Industry Road from Wudan to Baiyintaohai in Wengniute Banner, Chifeng City, Inner Mongolia Autonomous Region

2023年"十大最美农村路"
"Top 10 Most Beautiful Rural Roads" in 2023

辽宁省丹东市东港市农村公路
Rural Road in Donggang City, Dandong City, Liaoning Province

REVITALIZATION ROAD 振兴路

辽宁省大连市庄河市崔桂线
Cuigui Road in Zhuanghe City, Dalian City, Liaoning Province

崔桂线位于辽宁省大连市庄河市北部步云山乡与桂云花乡之间，是一条重要的旅游观光路、产业连接路。这条路一路蜿蜒、山河相伴、风景秀丽、路畅景美。沿途极富地域特色的满族风情绘画墙、优质贴心的公路休息区等，彰显了新时代文明乡风为乡村振兴注入的新兴文化力量。

Cuigui Road is located in the northern part of Zhuanghe city, Dalian city, Liaoning province. It is an important tourism road and industry connection road. This road is winding all the way, accompanied by mountains, rivers and beautiful scenery. Along the route, painting walls with regional characteristics of Manchu flavor, high-quality and intimate rest areas, etc., highlight the emerging cultural strength of rural revitalization in the new era.

黑龙江省双鸭山市尖山区双富村农村公路

Rural Road in Shuangfu Village, Jianshan District, Shuangyashan City, Heilongjiang Province

上海市浦东新区大治河农村公路群桥

Group Bridges on Rural Road along Dazhi River in Pudong New Area, Shanghai Municipality

上海市松江区新浜镇林赵路

Linzhao Road in Xinbang Town, Songjiang District, Shanghai Municipality

REVITALIZATION ROAD　振 兴 路

江苏省连云港市连云区大桅尖路

Daweijian Road in Lianyun District, Lianyungang City, Jiangsu Province

大桅尖路蜿蜒36道弯，如蛟龙盘踞、穿梭于崇山峻岭之中，首尾接入骨干路网，道路线形合理，道路主体、安防设施质量良好。一路走来，可赏漫山红叶枫树湾、清香淡雅云雾茶庄、法相庄严法起寺、禅意盎然悟道庵、匹练悬空船山飞瀑、海天一色大桅尖……

Daweijian Road has 36 curves. It looks like a dragon with its head and tail connected to the main road network. The geometry design of the road is reasonable. The main structure and safety facilities are of good quality.

浙江省杭州市淳安县淳杨线

Chunyang Road in Chun'an County, Hangzhou City, Zhejiang Province

"Top 10 Most Beautiful Rural Roads" in 2019

淳杨公路及绿道，坚持科学规划与生态治理并举，不仅极大改善了交通条件，更有机串起沿线酒店、驿站、景点；坚持开湖透气与林木郁闭结合，构建了独特的生态景观长廊，推动形成绿道经济、赛事经济、田园经济、低空经济等发展模式，带动了乡村经济的快速增长，成为乡村振兴的典范之作。

Chunyang Road and its greenway adhere to the simultaneous implementation of scientific planning and ecological governance, which not only greatly improves the traffic conditions, but also organically connects the hotels, post stations, and scenic spots along the route. It promotes the development of greenway economy, sports economy, rural economy and low-altitude economy, and has become a model for rural revitalization.

REVITALIZATION ROAD 振兴路

浙江省丽水市景宁畲族自治县农村公路

Rural Road in Jingning She Autonomous County, Lishui City, Zhejiang Province

丽水围绕"修一条路、造一片景、活一地经济、富一方百姓"的理念，通过提质扩面、创新赋能、路产协同等举措，高质量建设"四好农村路"，不仅改变了农村的面貌，打通了致富的渠道，更架起了一座党群的"连心桥"。"四好农村路"已经成为景宁畲族自治县乡村振兴的"必经之路"，成为广大农民脱贫攻坚建小康的"致富之路"，成为农民平安高效出行的"便捷之路"。

Lishui promotes the construction, management, maintenance and operation of roads in rural areas with high quality. Lishui has not only changed the appearance of rural areas and opened up channels to get rich, but also set up a "connecting bridge" between the Party and the people.

REVITALIZATION ROAD 振兴路

"Top 10 Most Beautiful Rural Roads" in 2021

江西省鹰潭市余江区大桥至司马源公路
Daqiao to Simayuan Road in Yujiang District, Yingtan City, Jiangxi Province

安徽省宣城市郎溪县农村公路
Rural Road in Langxi County, Xuancheng City, Anhui Province

大桥至司马源公路，蜿蜒于高公寨山水间，引领游客深入探索古桥、村落的秀美风光，更让红色文化资源焕发新生，以路为媒，将昔日闭塞的山乡与世界紧密相连，让勃勃生机在沿线乡村涌动。

Daqiao to Simayuan Road, winding in the Gaogongzhai landscape, not only leads tourists to deeply explore the beautiful scenery of the ancient bridge and the village, but also revitalizes the red culture resources.

福建省福州市鼓楼区农村公路
Rural Road in Gulou District, Fuzhou City, Fujian Province

2022年 "十大最美农村路"

"Top 10 Most Beautiful Rural Roads" in 2022

盘石—朱吴民俗旅游路，以 167 道弯著称，是 1962 年版电影《地雷战》的拍摄地，连接了盘石店与朱吴两镇，串联起许世友在胶东纪念馆、地雷战景区等全域旅游景点，沿线发展了乡村旅游、红色研学、生态康养、民宿集群等新兴产业，加速了文旅融合与乡村产业振兴，成为推动地方经济发展的新动脉。

The Folk Tourism Road from Panshi to Zhuwu, known for its 167 bends, connects the towns of Panshidian and Zhuwu. Along the route, emerging industries have flourished. It has accelerated the integration of culture and tourism and the revitalization of rural industries, emerging as a new driving force for local economic development.

山东省烟台市海阳市盘石—朱吴（民俗旅游路）
Panshi to Zhuwu Road (Folk Tourism Road) in Haiyang City, Yantai City, Shandong Province

河南省平顶山市鲁山县县道环湖路

Lake Road in Lushan County, Pingdingshan City, Henan Province

"Top 10 Most Beautiful Rural Roads" in 2022

鲁山县环湖路"三季有花、四季见绿",全线景色怡人,沿途昭平湖、皇姑浴温泉、环湖路高端民俗带、姑嫂石景点等遥相呼应、熠熠生辉,深受摄影爱好者和广大游客喜爱,被称为鲁山的"最美网红打卡地"。环湖路带动村民稳定增收、脱贫致富,已成为助力乡村经济腾飞的振兴之路。

The lake road in Lushan county has driven villagers to steadily increase their income and get rid of poverty, and has become a revitalization road to help the rural economy develop vigorously.

中国"四好农村路" RURAL ROADS IN CHINA

2022年
"十大最美农村路"

"Top 10 Most Beautiful Rural Roads"
in 2022

湖南省张家界市武陵源区插园公路
Chayuan Road in Wulingyuan Scenic Area, Zhangjiajie City, Hunan Province

武陵源区插园公路是环景区公路南线的一部分，沿线建设彩虹护栏，融合了音乐、绘画等人文元素，并打造慢行系统和夜光游道，促进了乡村旅游和经济发展。

Chayuan Road is part of the southern route of the road around Wulingyuan Scenic Area. A rainbow guardrail has been constructed along the road, which combines music, paintings and other human elements. The road has also been constructed with the slow-moving traffic system and the glow-in-the-dark walkway. It promotes rural tourism and economic development.

湖北省宜昌市夷陵区农村公路
Rural Road in Yiling District, Yichang City, Hubei Province

中国"四好农村路" RURAL ROADS IN CHINA

湖南省张家界市永定区农村公路
Rural Road in Yongding District, Zhangjiajie City, Hunan Province

广东省韶关市仁化县阅丹公路

Yuedan Road in Renhua County, Shaoguan City, Guangdong Province

广西壮族自治区河池市都安瑶族自治县"蛇形公路"
"Snake Shaped Road" in Du'an Yao Autonomous County, Hechi City, Guangxi Zhuang Autonomous Region

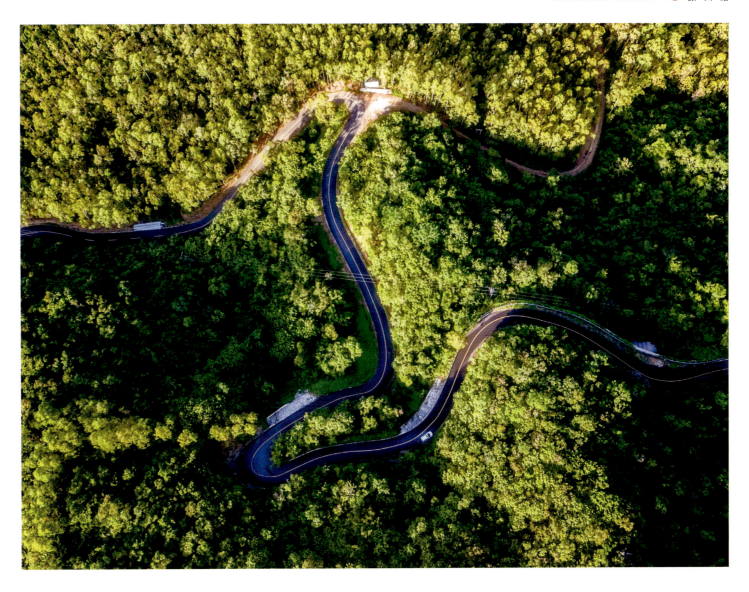

海南省东方市农村公路（大广坝至俄贤岭公路）
Rural Road (from Daguangba to Exianling) in Dongfang City, Hainan Province

中国"四好农村路" RURAL ROADS IN CHINA

"Top 10 Most Beautiful Rural Roads" in 2023

重庆市铜梁区铜梁乡村振兴西郊示范片公路
Road in Xijiao Demonstration Area, Tongliang District, Chongqing Municipality

西郊示范片公路串起了城市与乡村、美景与产业，推动农区变景区、田园变花园，将沿线优质水果、精品水产、花卉苗木、有机蔬菜、生态莲藕等产业基地和玄天秀水生态画廊、奇彩梦园、荷和原乡等景区景点串连起来，让大美乡村内外兼修、形神兼具，呈现出"产业兴旺、生态宜居、乡风文明、治理有效、生活富裕"的乡村振兴美丽画卷。

The road in Xijiao demonstration area strings up the city and the countryside, as well as beautiful scenery and industry. Along the road, there are industry bases and many tourist attractions. The road presents a beautiful picture of rural revitalization with "prosperous industry, ecological livability, civilized rural customs, effective governance and rich living".

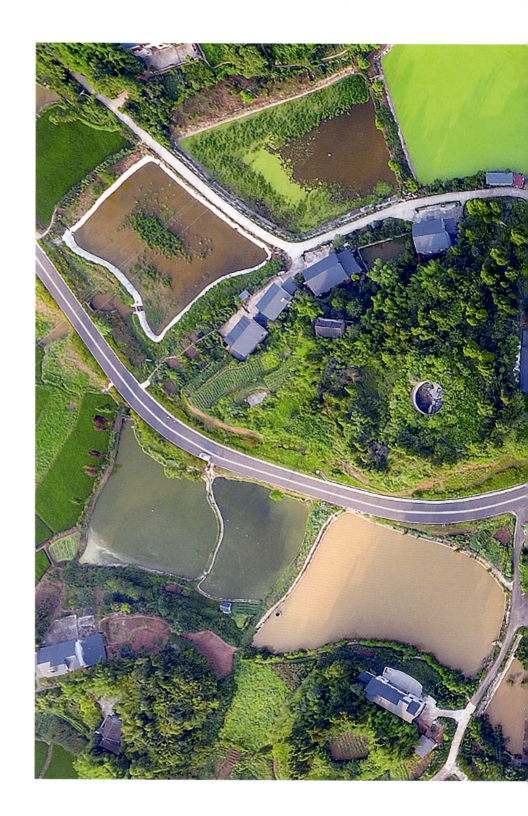

REVITALIZATION ROAD 振 兴 路

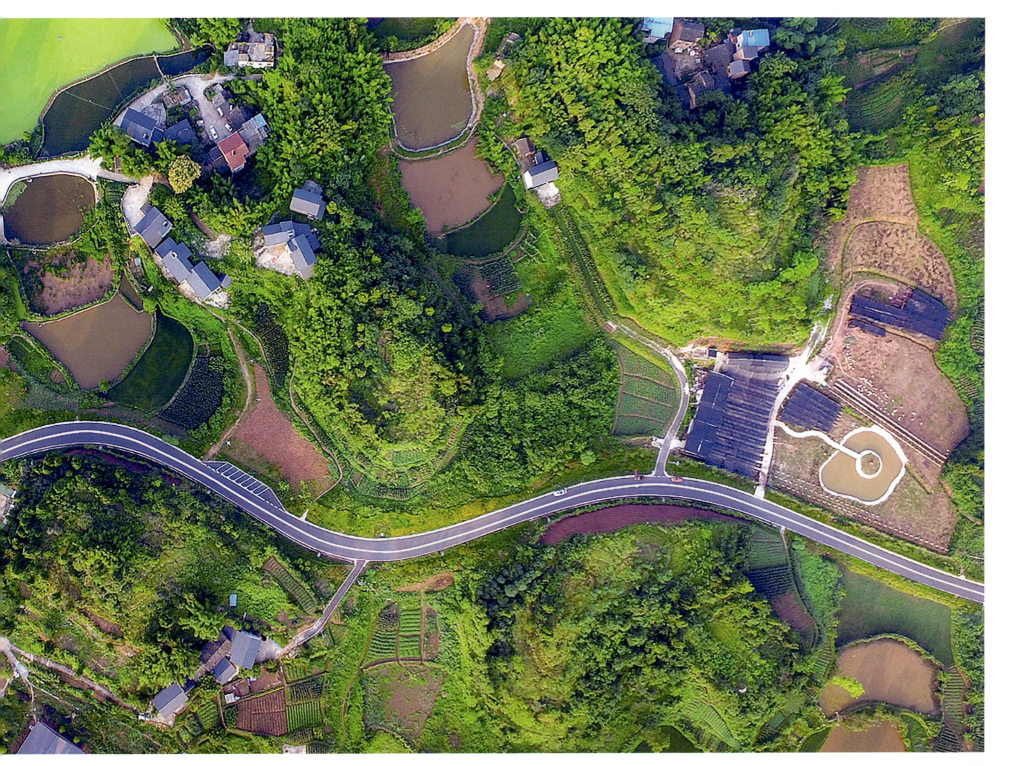

四川省雅安市荥经县龙苍沟熊猫翠竹长廊

Longcanggou Panda Bambo Corridor in Yingjing County, Ya'an City, Sichuan Province

熊猫翠竹长廊以路为线，贯穿大熊猫国家公园"三大圈层"，连通入口社区"五大重点"，撬动百亿旅游产业在此蓬勃发展，实现了从"绿水青山"向"金山银山"转变，是国家公园体系共建共享、人与自然和谐共生、路旅路产融合发展的乡村振兴典范。

The Panda Bamboo Corridor runs through the "three circles" of the Giant Panda National Park, connects the "five key points" of the entrance community, and promotes the development of the tourism industry. It is a model of rural revitalization.

"Top 10 Most Beautiful Rural Roads" in 2021

四川省成都市蒲江县青山铁牛旅游环线
Qingshan Tieniu Tourism Ring Road in Pujiang County, Chengdu City, Sichuan Province

青山铁牛旅游环线串联起了铁牛水乡、西来古镇、成都战役纪念馆、临溪河等人文和自然景观，打通了乡村振兴与农民增收致富的快速通道，沿线因路而变、因路而美、因路而兴，改善了沿线群众的出行条件，带动了沿线乡村旅游、红色旅游、观光农业的高速发展以及传统文化的传承和保护，成为一条名副其实的产业路、景观路、致富路，真正实现了"交通+"的多元化发展。

Qingshan Tieniu tourism ring road connects human and natural sceneries, and opens up a fast channel for rural revitalization and farmers' income and wealth. The road has improved the travelling conditions of the people along the road, and driven the rapid development of rural tourism, red tourism, and sightseeing agriculture as well as the inheritance and protection of traditional culture. It has truly realized the diversified development of "Transportation Plus".

四川省甘孜藏族自治州色达县五色海旅游环线
Wusehai Tourism Ring Road in Seda County,
Garze Tibetan Autonomous Prefecture, Sichuan Province

"Top 10 Most Beautiful Rural Roads" in 2023

　　五色海旅游环线公路，作为甘孜藏族自治州的经济动脉与文化桥梁，不仅极大地提升了区域交通便捷性，更促进了旅游业的繁荣与农牧民增收。公路途经地区具有壮丽独特的自然景观和深厚的藏族文化，畅行其中，游客可以领略自然奇观与文化底蕴的完美融合。

As the economic artery and cultural bridge of Garze Tibetan Autonomous Prefecture, the Wusehai tourism ring road has not only greatly enhanced the regional transportation convenience, but also promoted the prosperity of tourism and the income increase of farmers and herdsmen. The road passes through areas with magnificent and unique natural landscape as well as profound Tibetan culture, in which tourists can enjoy the perfect fusion of natural wonders and cultural heritage.

REVITALIZATION ROAD 振 兴 路

贵州省黔南布依族苗族自治州都匀市农村公路
Rural Road in Duyun City, Qiannan Buyi and Miao Autonomous Prefecture, Guizhou Province

云南省昭通市绥江县乡村公路

Rural Road in Suijiang County, Zhaotong City, Yunnan Province

西藏自治区山南市浪卡子县羊卓雍错景区公路
Road in Yamdroktso Scenic Area, Nagarze County, Shannan City, Xizang Autonomous Region

陕西省延安市宜川县凤马路
Fengma Road in Yichuan County, Yan'an City, Shaanxi Province

中国"四好农村路" RURAL ROADS IN CHINA

甘肃省白银市景泰县农村公路

Rural Road in Jingtai County, Baiyin City, Gansu Province

青海省海北藏族自治州祁连县农村公路
Rural Road in Qilian County, Haibei Tibetan Autonomous Prefecture, Qinghai Province

中国"四好农村路" RURAL ROADS IN CHINA

REVITALIZATION ROAD 振 兴 路

青海省海北藏族自治州门源回族自治县农村公路
Rural Road in Menyuan Hui Autonomous County, Haibei Tibetan Autonomous Prefecture, Qinghai Province

中国"四好农村路" RURAL ROADS IN CHINA

宁夏回族自治区中卫市海原县农村公路
Rural Road in Haiyuan County, Zhongwei City, Ningxia Hui Autonomous Region

中国"四好农村路" RURAL ROADS IN CHINA

新疆维吾尔自治区喀什地区塔什库尔干塔吉克自治县盘龙古道

Panlong Ancient Road in Tashkurgan Tajik Autonomous County, Kashgar Prefecture, Xinjiang Uygur Autonomous Region

新疆维吾尔自治区阿克苏地区柯坪县盖孜力克镇色热克托格热克村—苏贝西村（Y534）
Y534 Road in Gaizilike Town, Keping County, Aksu Prefecture, Xinjiang Uygur Autonomous Region

"Top 10 Most Beautiful Rural Roads" in 2022

盖孜力克镇色热克托格热克村—苏贝西村(Y534)公路全长14.679公里，沿途能够欣赏到戈壁、水库、风化岩石等特色景观。这条路方便了群众出行、带动了农产品运输、推动了产业发展，是一条民心路、幸福路、振兴路。

The total length of Y534 Road is 14.679 kilometers. Along the road, we can enjoy the characteristic sceneries of the Gobi Desert, reservoirs, and weathered rocks, etc. This road facilitates the travelling of local people, drives the transportation of agricultural products and promotes the development of industries.

后 记

为展示奋力加快建设交通强国，努力当好中国式现代化开路先锋的成就，让国内外更好地了解中国交通发展，我们策划出版了"中国交通名片丛书"。其中，《中国"四好农村路"》分册得到了交通运输部政策研究室、公路局的大力支持。

本书编写力求科学严谨、求真务实。中国公路杂志社提供了大量图片和文字素材，中国交通报社等单位提出了很多建设性意见。

编写出版过程中，北京、内蒙古、吉林、黑龙江、上海、浙江、江西、山东、河南、湖南、广东、海南、重庆、四川、云南、陕西、甘肃、宁夏等地交通运输主管部门提出了很多好的意见和建议。

人民交通出版社对本书的出版非常重视，社领导舒驰、刘韬、陈志敏多次提出宝贵意见，吴有铭、刘永超、黎小东、丁遥、师静圆等同志为本书编辑做了大量工作。

经过 10 年的高质量发展，中国"四好农村路"取得了举世瞩目的发展成就，农民群众获得感、幸福感、安全感不断增强，农村公路成为老百姓家门口的致富路、幸福路、连心路、振兴路。"四好农村路"已成为一张亮丽的"中国名片"。受编写资料和篇幅所限，本书难免挂一漏万，存在不足之处，欢迎广大读者提出宝贵意见、建议，便于我们及时修订完善，以期更好地宣传好、展示好这张"中国名片"！

编者

2024 年 9 月

EPILOGUE

In order to show the achievements of building China into a country with great transport strength and being the trailblazer in China's modernization drive, and enable domestic and international readers to better understand China's transport development, we have planned and published the "Card Book Series: Transport in China". Among them, the volume titled "Rural Roads in China" has received strong support from the Policy Research Office and the Highway Department of the Ministry of Transport.

When compiling this book, we strive to be scientifically rigorous, realistic and pragmatic. China Highway Magazine provided a wealth of pictures and text materials, and China Transport News and other units put forward many constructive suggestions.

During the compilation and publication process, the transport authorities in Beijing, Inner Mongolia, Jilin, Heilongjiang, Shanghai, Zhejiang, Jiangxi, Shandong, Henan, Hunan, Guangdong, Hainan, Chongqing, Sichuan, Yunnan, Shaanxi, Gansu, Ningxia, and other places put forward many good opinions and suggestions.

China Communications Press attaches great importance to the publication of this book, and its management Shu Chi, Liu Tao, and Chen Zhimin have offered valuable opinions and suggestions on multiple occasions. Wu Youming, Liu Yongchao, Li Xiaodong, Ding Yao, Shi Jingyuan and other colleagues did a lot of work for the editing of this book.

After 10 years of high-quality development, the construction, management, maintenance and operation of roads in rural areas have made remarkable development achievements in China that have attracted worldwide attention. The sense of gain, happiness, and security of farmers has continued to increase, and rural roads have become the roads to prosperity, happiness, unity, and revitalization right at people's doorsteps. These rural roads have become a brilliant "business card of China". Due to the limitation of compilation materials and space, there are inevitably some deficiencies in this book. We welcome readers to put forward valuable opinions and suggestions so that we can revise and improve it in time and better display this "business card of China".

Editors
September 2024

图书在版编目（CIP）数据

中国"四好农村路"：汉文、英文 /《中国"四好农村路"》编写组编. — 北京：人民交通出版社股份有限公司, 2024. 10. — ISBN 978-7-114-19727-7

Ⅰ. F542.3-64

中国国家版本馆 CIP 数据核字第 2024S86F84 号

本书由人民交通出版社独家出版发行。未经著作权人书面许可，本书图片及文字任何部分，不得以任何方式和手段进行复制、转载或刊登。版权所有，侵权必究。

Copyright © 2024

All rights reserved. No part of this publication may be reproduced, stored in a retrieval system, or transmitted in any form or by any means, electronic, mechanical, photocopying, recording or otherwise, without the prior written permission of the copyright holder. Printed in China.

Zhongguo "Si Hao Nongcun Lu"

书　　名：	中国"四好农村路"
著　作　者：	《中国"四好农村路"》编写组
责任编辑：	吴有铭　刘永超　黎小东　丁　遥
责任校对：	赵媛媛　龙　雪
责任印制：	张　凯
出版发行：	人民交通出版社
地　　址：	（100011）北京市朝阳区安定门外外馆斜街3号
网　　址：	http://www.ccpcl.com.cn
销售电话：	（010）85285857
总 经 销：	人民交通出版社发行部
经　　销：	各地新华书店
印　　刷：	北京雅昌艺术印刷有限公司
开　　本：	965×635　1/8
印　　张：	24.5
字　　数：	244千
版　　次：	2024年10月　第1版
印　　次：	2024年10月　第1次印刷
书　　号：	ISBN 978-7-114-19727-7
定　　价：	368.00元

（有印刷、装订质量问题的图书，由本社负责调换）